590   Lewin, Ted
LEW   What am I? where am I?

DATE DUE			
FE 1 4 '14			
MR 2 1 '14			
JUN 7 9 2015			
FEB 1 7 2016			

What Am I?
Where Am I?

by Ted Lewin

Holiday House / New York

To Dan'l and Susan

I LIKE TO READ is a registered trademark of Holiday House, Inc.

Copyright © 2013 by Ted Lewin
All Rights Reserved
HOLIDAY HOUSE is registered in the U.S. Patent and Trademark Office.
Printed and Bound in April 2013 at Tien Wah Press, Johor Bahru, Johor, Malaysia.
The text typeface is Report School.
The artwork was created with pencil, watercolor,
and liquid mask on Strathmore bristol.
www.holidayhouse.com
First Edition
1 3 5 7 9 10 8 6 4 2

Library of Congress Cataloging-in-Publication Data
Lewin, Ted.
What am I? where am I? / by Ted Lewin. — First edition.
pages cm. — (I like to read)
ISBN 978-0-8234-2856-4 (hardcover)
1. Animals—Juvenile literature.
2. Habitat (Ecology)—Juvenile literature. I. Title.
QL49.L3878 2013
590—dc23
2012039289

What am I?

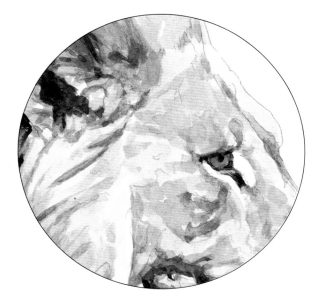

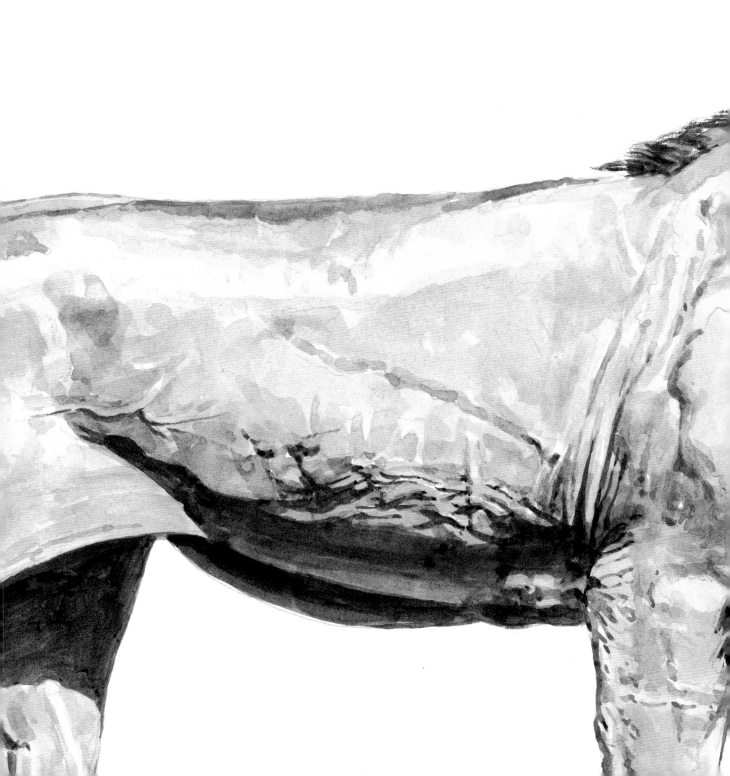

I am a lion.
Where am I?

I am a reindeer.
Where am I?

I am in the tundra.

What am I?

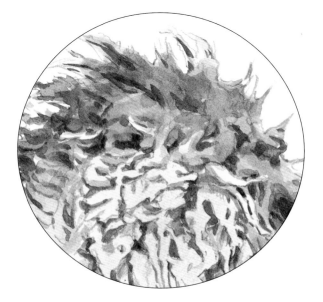

I am a camel.
Where am I?

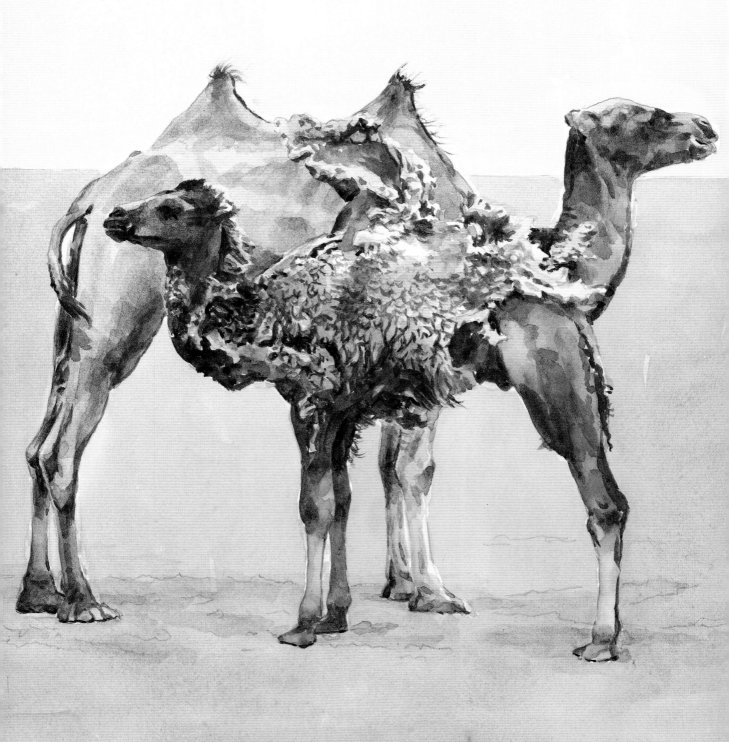

I am in the desert.

What am I?

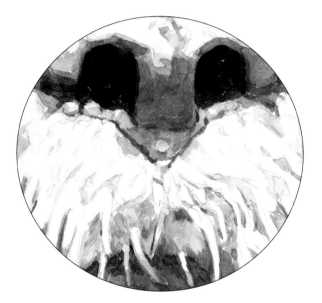

I am in water.

What am I?

I am a tiger.
Where am I?

I am in a forest.

What am I?
I am a boy.
I am on the beautiful earth.

I Like to Read® Books
You will like all of them!

Boy, Bird, and Dog by David McPhail

Car Goes Far by Michael Garland

Come Back, Ben by Ann Hassett and John Hassett

Dinosaurs Don't, Dinosaurs Do by Steve Björkman

Fireman Fred by Lynn Rowe Reed

Fish Had a Wish by Michael Garland

The Fly Flew In by David Catrow

Happy Cat by Steve Henry

I Have a Garden by Bob Barner

I Will Try by Marilyn Janovitz

Late Nate in a Race by Emily Arnold McCully

The Lion and the Mice
by Rebecca Emberley and Ed Emberley

Look! by Ted Lewin

Me Too! by Valeri Gorbachev

Mice on Ice
by Rebecca Emberley and Ed Emberley

Pete Won't Eat by Emily Arnold McCully

Pig Has a Plan by Ethan Long

Sam and the Big Kids by Emily Arnold McCully

See Me Dig by Paul Meisel

See Me Run by Paul Meisel
A THEODOR SEUSS GEISEL AWARD HONOR BOOK

Sick Day by David McPhail

What Am I? Where Am I? by Ted Lewin

You Can Do It! by Betsy Lewin

Visit holidayhouse.com to learn more
about I Like to Read® Books.